PROCEEDINGS

AND

ADDRESS,

OF THE

Democratic State Convention,

HELD AT

SYRACUSE,

JANUARY TENTH AND ELEVENTH,

1856.

ALBANY;
1856.

PROCEEDINGS.

Pursuant to the call of the Democratic State Central Committee, the delegates from the several Assembly Districts met at noon on the 10th day of January, A. D. 1856, in the City Hall, in the city of Syracuse.

Mr. BALLARD, of Cortland, called the Convention to order, and on his motion, Hon. JOHN J. TAYLOR, of Tioga, was appointed temporary chairman.

Mr. TAYLOR, on taking the chair, addressed the Convention as follows:

GENTLEMEN OF THE CONVENTION:

Accept my thanks for the distinguished honor you have conferred upon me in inviting me to preside over your incipient proceedings. I do not deem this a proper occasion to make an address, nor is it necessary that I should. You are all aware of the duties we have to discharge, in expressing the sentiments of the democrats of this state, and in selecting delegates to represent them in the National Convention. I trust we shall each feel the responsibility of these duties and hope we shall so discharge them as to have the approbation of our own consciences and the approval of our constituents. Let us so shape our action that it will be in accordance with sound national principles, and tend to secure equal rights to every portion of our country.

Mr. BROWN, of Jefferson, and Mr. CLINTON, of Erie, were appointed temporary Secretaries.

On motion, the counties were called, when the following delegates appeared:

Albany..........Jas. M. Kimball, H. H. Van Dyck, Nicholas Hill, Jr., Francis Kearney.

Allegany.........L. P. Weatherby, J. M. Mott.

Broome..........O. C. Crocker.

Cattaraugus.....G. S. Hickox, Patrick Short.

Cayuga.........J. N. Knapp, John L. Parker, D. S. Titus.

Chautauque......L. B. Smith, Samuel W. Bagnell.

Chemung........William R. Judson.

Chenango........S. S. Meritt, Horace Packer.

Columbia........William A. Carpenter, Thomas M. Burt.

Cortland.........Horatio Ballard.

Delaware........O. M. Allaben, Charles Maples.

Dutchess........Gilbert Dean, Joseph Martin.

Erie............Israel T. Hatch, Allen Potter, H. P. Clinton, M. R. Loveland.

Fulton & Hamilton Daniel Smith.

Genesee..........Dean Richmond, F. M. Craig.

Herkimer........George W. Pine, George B. Judd.

Jefferson.........Levi H. Brown, Charles K. Loomis.

Kings...........S. E. Johnson, Wm. Marion, D. D. Briggs, D. A. Wright.

Livingston.......William C. Hawley, James Faulkner.

Madison.........S. T. Fairchild.

Monroe..........Jas. C. Campbell, Justus Yale, S. B. Jewett.

Montgomery......Francis Newkirk, David Spraker.

New York.......Michael Murray, P. Matthews, George H. Purser, L. Harrison Smith, Thomas W. Adams, Albert Smith, George W. Roome, Asahel Reed, Hiram Engle, Benj. P. Fairchild, E. C. McConnell, Henry P. West, Daniel W. Norris, John Cochrane, L. B. Shepard.

Niagara.........William Vandevoort, A. V. E. Hotchkiss.

Oneida..........George Graham, J. Thomas Spriggs.

Onondaga.......C. B. Wheeler, John M. Strong, Charles F. Williston, Wm. Taylor.

Ontario.........Myron H. Peck.

Orange..........D. E. Fowler, C. S. Potter.

Oswego..........Benjamin E. Bowen.

Otsego..........Charles McLean, Daniel V. Boden.

Putnam.........A. Prince.

Queens..........Manus Kelly.

Rensselaer.......A. McConihe, William Harrington, Gilbert Westfall.

Richmond.......Thomas Burns.

St. Lawrence.....R. W. Judson, John L. Russell, Noble S. Elderkin.
Seneca ....Josiah T. Miller.
Steuben ....T. N. McCabe.
Suffolk..........William H. Ludlow.
Schenectady ......Nich. Vandebogart & Alex. J. Thompson—Contestants.
Sullivan ....F. A. Devoe.
Tioga...........John J. Taylor.
Tompkins........Lewis Vankirk, H. D. Barto, Jr.
Ulster...........Peter Rowe, T. R. Westbrook.
Washington .....Atherton Hall.
Wayne..........George W. Paddock, Pomeroy Tucker.
Westchester ......E. J. Horton, George W. Ditchet.
Wyoming ....T. S. Cushing.
Yates ....L. S. Ayres.

The county of Schenectady, the 14th District of New York, and one district from the county of Kings, were found to be contested, whereupon

On motion of Mr. PURSER, of New York, a committee of five upon contested seats was appointed.

On motion of Mr. BALLARD, of Cortland, it was ordered that a committee of one from each judicial district, be appointed to report permanent officers.

The Chair announced the following committee on contested seats:—Messrs. PURSER, WESTBROOK, CAMPBELL, MERRITT, JUDSON.

Committee on Organization:—Messrs. ROOME, 1st; MARTIN, 2d; HARRINGTON, 3d; HALL, 4th; LUDINGTON, 5th; BALLARD, 6th; HAWLEY, 7th; POTTER, 8th.

Mr. COCHRANE, of New York, moved that the rules of the late Assembly be the rules of the Convention. Carried.

On motion of Mr. JEWETT, the Convention adjourned to 3 P. M.

THREE O'CLOCK, P. M.

The Convention re-assembled, pursuant to adjournment.

Mr. BALLARD, from the committee for that purpose, submitted the following officers for the permanent organization of the Convention:

President—WILLIAM H. LUDLOW.

Vice Presidents — George H. Purser, Joseph Martin, Alonzo McConihe, John L. Russell, George B. Judd, Charles McLean, Jamel Faulkner, A. V. E. Hotchkiss.

Secretaries — Levi H. Brown, H. P. Clinton, Hiram Engle, Horace Packer.

The President, on taking the Chair, spoke as follows :

I thank you, gentlemen, for the honorable position you have assigned to me. Rest assured, that to the full extent of my ability, I shall impartially discharge the duties of the Chair.

Gentlemen, you have here assembled under circumstances of great and vital interest. You are now on the eve of an important National Convention, and you are called on at this time, not only to make judicious selections of delegates to that Convention, but you are also called on to lay down a platform of principles, which shall truly represent the Democracy of our State, and which at this period of political chaos, shall proclaim to the Democratic brotherhood of the Union, where the Democracy of New York stand, what they mean and what they want.

Gentlemen, it is my most earnest desire that wisdom and moderation may guide your counsels, and that their result may be alike acceptable to yourselves, and to the constituencies whom you severally represent.

And gentlemen, it is my most earnest further desire, that the delegates from the Empire State may meet their co-laborers at Cincinnati, on a footing of proud equality. I am confident that no act of this Convention will compromise that attitude.

Mr. Dean, of Dutchess, moved the appointment of a committee of sixteen to report an Address and resolutions. The motion was adopted.

Mr. Jewett, of Monroe, moved the appointment of a committee of sixteen—two from each Judicial District—to report a list of delegates to the Democratic National Convention. Carried.

Mr. Cochrane, of New York, moved to adjourn until 7 P. M. Carried.

EVENING SESSION.

The Convention met at 7 o'clock.

The Chair annnounced the following committees:

ADDRESS AND RESOLUTIONS.

District.

1—Cochrane and Shepard, of New York.
2—Dean, of Dutchess, and Briggs, of Kings.
3—Hill, of Albany, and Westbrook, of Ulster.
4—Spraker, of Montgomery, and Russell, of St. Lawrence.
5—Loomis, of Jefferson, and Taylor, of Onondaga.
6—Fairchild, of Madison, and Taylor, of Tioga.
7—Tucker, of Wayne, and McKay, of Steuben.
8—Potter, of Orleans, and Wetherby, of Allegany.

ON SELECTION OF DELEGATES TO THE NATIONAL CONVENTION.

District.

1—Norris and Adams, New York.
2—Wright, of Kings, and Fowler, of Orange.
3—Westfall, of Rensselaer, and Carpenter, of Columbia.
4—Judson, of St. Lawrence, and Newkirk, of Montgomery.
5—Graham, of Oneida, and Woolworth, of Lewis.
6—Merritt, of Chenango, and Crocker, of Broome.
7—Jewett, of Monroe, and Titus, of Cayuga.
8—Richmond, of Genesee, and Vandervoort, of Niagara.

The Convention then took a recess to await the reports of the committees.

On the re-assembling of the Convention,

Mr. Purser read the report of the committee on contested seats in the New York cases, and Mr. Westbrook in the Schenectady case.

The committee arrived at the following results:

First and Third Districts, New York—That the Contestants, S. E. Johnson and Marius Kelly, had magnanimously withdrawn in favor of Messrs. D. A. Wright and William Marion.

Tenth District, New York—That Mr. Fairchild is entitled to the seat instead of Mr. Swackhammer.

Fourteenth District, New York—That the committee cannot decide between the contestants, and reports a vacancy in this seat.

Schenectady County—That neither side is strictly regular, and that both contestants be admitted to seats, with power to cast one vote.

The question being on the report of the committee, a division was called for, and the Chair stated that the question would be put on each case separately.

The case of the 10th district in New York being taken up, the contestants, Messrs. SWACKHAMMER and FAIRCHILD, were heard.

A motion was made to amend by admitting both delegates.

The amendment was rejected and the report of the committee agreed to.

In the case of the 14th district in New York, the report of the committee was agreed to.

The Schenectady case coming up, Mr. BALLARD stating that he understood the committee to report that neither side was regular, moved to amend so that both delegates be rejected.

A discussion ensued, and various motions and amendments were proposed, when, under the previous question, the Convention was brought to a vote on the report, and it was rejected.

A motion of Mr. BALLARD to reject both claimants was then adopted.

The Convention then took a recess till 10 o'clock, to hear the report of the committee on resolutions.

TEN O'CLOCK P. M.

Mr. HILL, of Albany, from the committee for that purpose, reported the following Address :

ADDRESS.

Fellow Citizens :—

We address you in the name of the Democratic Party. Our reflections, uniting with the experience of the past, have satisfied us that the prosperity of the country depends upon the permanent ascendancy of democratic principles. Whether we are right in this you must judge. If not, we have erred with some of the wisest patriots and statesmen that ever lived. We are far from claiming that the Democratic Party has never gone astray, or that all good men have adopted its faith. Good men have sometimes opposed it, but we think from mistaken views ; and bad men have sometimes joined it under a like delusion. What we claim for it is, that its political creed is in harmony with the true spirit of our institutions, and that it cannot fail in upholding them while it keeps near the light of its own principles. We invite your attention to some considerations on this subject.

The Democratic Party was designed merely as a means of influencing the course of public or governmental affairs, by the concentrated action of political opinion ; leaving all other matters to the free and unbiassed choice of the citizen. It was not organized, as some of its former professed friends seem to have assumed, to keep watch and ward over the entire domain of taste and sentiment, thought and duty ; or to act as a spy upon the private opinions or pursuits of men, or sit in judgment upon their consciences, or control even their outward conduct, except through the rightful action of government. These are heresies of modern growth, entirely alien to the principles for which the illustrious defenders of our faith, with Jefferson at their head, steadfastly contended in former years. Their objects were purely governmental in their nature, and their political creed, though broad enough to reach every subject of governmental concern, extended no farther. On other subjects, where government could not or should not act, their creed was either silent, or spoke only to admonish us of the duty of forbearance, and the danger of interfering. It was fashioned, indeed, with most wise and cautious reference to the true principles of regulated liberty; proscribing no one for the opinions he held, the altar at which he worshipped, or the place where he was born; and countenancing no tyranny over him in any of his private relations. For it was the creed of men who, with arms in their hands, had just rebuked the unrighteous intermeddling of one Usurper, and feared that another might succeed; men who had read history, and knew how surely this evil spirit of tyrannical encroachment lurks in the shadow of power; and how it destroys the energy of the citizen, wastes the springs of public action, and eradicates from whole communities the virtues of self-dependence, courage and patriotism. If the past has left any admonition for the present which should be heeded by every statesman and every friend of the country, it is that the powers of States and Nations have been pressed beyond due limits; and that the business of governing men, by organic public force, has been overdone. This truth is deeply graven in the history of those Nations which have compelled their subjects to submit for centuries to minute police regulations, until they ceased to rely, not only on themselves, but almost on Providence; and looked listlessly to government as the fountain of morals, religion, right and duty—the author and finisher of all things. Its importance is attested by all those limitations upon governmental action so carefully prescribed in our written constitutions; and the democratic creed, in view of the never-ceasing tendencies of power to enlarge itself, warns us that unslumbering, nay, "eternal vigilance, is the price of liberty."

The disregard of these admonitory lessons, gleaned from the bitter experience of the past, has betrayed many into erroneous views of the true objects of political association, and the appropriate functions of government; errors harmless enough while they remain mere speculations of the closet, but which are found eminently mischievous in practice. Without adverting at present to other illustrations, let us turn for a moment to the course which some now invite us to take with regard to the subject of domestic slavery. More than once during the period of our national existence, the efforts of men professing unbounded sympathy for the slave, to induce government to act in furtherance of their theories, forgetful of every other object of political association, have given just cause for serious alarm. And recently, nay within the last few months, other men, with loud professions of democracy on their lips, while their hearts are far from it, have banded themselves for renewed and more formidable efforts to evoke the spirit of Abolitionism, with all the gloomy passions which wait on it. This last organization was deemed so important by its authors and abettors, as to call for the instant abandonment of every other political creed, and its advent was accordingly ushered in by a formal resolution announcing that the Whig and Democratic parties were to exist no longer ; that henceforward there were to be no more Whigs nor Democrats, but that all were to be ANTI-SLAVERY REPUBLICANS. Nor was the surprise excited by this announcement at all diminished when we were told in effect afterward, by the Chief Captain of the new forces thus mustered against the peace of the Union, that the owners of slaves were to be treated as an odious "Aristocracy," which "in every case and throughout all hazards, should be abhorred and avoided ;" that the interests of the North and South, were therefore directly and irreconcilably antagonistic ; that the citizens of these different sections of our common country could no longer dwell together in unity ; that the compromises of the constitution were a hollow truce which had been kept too long ; that Congress must be urged to set them at defiance, and assume uncompromising, aggressive, anti-slavery ground ; and that every other effort of government must be subordinated to this, and every other test of political faith at once abandoned ! And to remove all doubt from our minds, as to the temper and resolution with which the warfare was to be waged, we were told a little later, through the columns of a leading paper devoted to the cause, that the South was about to be called into fearful account; not "for commerce, but for *vengeance !*"

When we consider that these avowals were made in the name of what now claims to be a great party, and that they were not uttered in the heat of blood, but prepared for the public eye after consultation and deliberation, they invest the subject with a solemn and startling interest, and may well excite gloomy forebodings as to the future. The time is come, fellow-citizens, when the ground on which we stand should be carefully examined, and the course we are to take in the coming struggle clearly delineated and understood.

Without pausing to inquire here whether Congress has power to act in accordance with the views of this new sect—a question which admits of no answer but an unhesitating negative, if we rightly appreciate the tendency of their doctrines—we pass to the more practical and broader inquiry whether it *ought* to adopt them ? Let us give these men the benefit of their disclaimers. Let us admit that they do not propose to interfere with slavery now in either of the old thirteen states ; that they intend no insult to their brethern of those states, while branding them as objects of governmental distrust and abhorence ; that they are athirst for peace and tranquility, while invoking the demons of discord and strife ; that they venerate the Union, while denouncing the wisdom which framed it as "treason against humanity ;" and that they hope to perpetuate its blessings by joining hands with them who hate and curse it and pray for its overthrow. Grant that all of them do not see the tendency of their actions, or the inevitable end of their career, and that they are doing this evil with a vague expectation that some possible good may come at last. Still, the question is not what they intend or ultimately expect, but what course should others take whose sense of duty is yet unsubdued by the frenzy of fanaticism or the lust of power ? Is it wise, is it just, is it right in any conceivable view—nay, is it not both absurd and criminal—to countenance the theories which now, for the first time in our national history, this motley throng of politicians claim shall be enforced, "in every case and throughout all hazards," by direct governmental action.

We have assumed that they are not yet so far gone in delusion as to meditate any present assault upon slavery in the old thirteen states ; though even this is but an inference, perhaps an unwarranted one, from their silence. In the strange document called their "platform of principles," drawn up by a professed abolitionist, and unanimously adopted as the permanent basis of their organization, we find the following distinct avowals, which show how wide a field of agitation they mean ultimately to occupy, and how little they are disposed to restrict it out of deference to the constitution :—

"*Resolved*, That the federal government, being one of defined and limited "powers &c.,we most earnestly deny its right to establish, uphold or *tolerate* "slavery in any portion of the public domain, or to *connive* at its existence in "the federal territory by any means whatever.

"*Resolved*, That since there *can* be no legal slavery in the Territories of our "Union, there *can be no slave States legally formed out of such Territories*," &c.

The powers of the general government in respect to slavery are the same to day that they were when the Union was formed, and if they have not been exceeded heretofore by the admission of slave states, they cannot be hereafter, In other words, if Congress has no power to admit new slave states now, as these theorists broadly affirm, it has had none at any time, and every act of that nature, whether past or future, may be treated as a mere usurpation, not obligatory upon any one. Suppose the cardinal doctrines inculcated by the resolutions we have quoted to be adopted as an elementary portion of our national policy, and to have become, what their authors mean they shall be, "the creed of political faith, the text of civic instruction, the touchstone by which to try the services of those we trust ;" at once the prompter and the guide of individual duty and public action. Everything hitherto done under which new slave States have been formed out of territory once constituting part of the public domain, must be then deemed unconstitutional, and therefore absolutely invalid for any practical end. Louisiana, Missouri, and all other States received into the Union in violation of the dogma on which alone resistance for the future is to be based, have none of the rights of States under the Confederacy ! If they are considered members of it for any purpose, they hold their position by sufferance only ; not in virtue of the constitution ! They are not entitled to be represented in the councils of the Nation, nor to its aid in suppressing domestic insurrection, or in repelling foreign invasion ; and every faithful believer in this new creed is bound to say so by his votes, in Congress and out of it ! Indeed, we are told that they have not a "republican form of government ;" that they are uncongenial and therefore unfit associates for the free States ; that they are mere "Aristocracies," which "in every case and *throughout all hazards*, must be abhorred and avoided;" and so they should be thrust from the Union, or compelled to change their domestic policy! Such, fellow-citizens, are some of the teachings of Anti-Slavery Republicanism. Such the broad and dismal field of agitation which it opens to our view, and on which it urges government to enter.

The problem of domestic slavery was one of the most delicate and difficult which the framers of the federal constitution had to solve. The institution then existed in nearly all the States, including New York; and was deeply interwoven with the social habits and industrial pursuits of our people. It had been fastened upon us by the coercive policy of the mother country, undeviatingly and perseveringly pursued through an hundred years; and one question was, whether it was compatible with that "republican form of government" which the United States were about to "guaranty to every State in this Union." If it was not, no Union could be formed, and the hopes and aspirations of the patriots who looked upon this as essential to complete the great work of the Revolution, and secure its fruits, must perish. Our fathers, with Washington as their presiding officer, deliberated upon it, not in the spirit of Anti-Slavery Republicanism, but like men on whose decision hung the fate of a Nation; invoking the spirit of peace, of mutual forbearance, conciliation and compromise. They balanced the countless practical and certain advantages of Union, against the vain hope of theoretical perfection in government, and our present constitution is the fortunate result of their decision. No one who believes that their decision was wise, and thanks God for bringing their counsels to such a termination, can consistently say that a "republican form of government" is incompatible with the toleration of American slavery. And no one we believe will say so, who truly reveres the constitution, and meditates no assault, now or hereafter, on its benificent adjustments and wise compromises.

The Anti-Slavery Republican Party, however, invites us to aid in giving ascendancy to men who have said and do say so, and who strive to make their dogmas the foundation of governmental action, as well as the test and limit of political faith. Men who, had they stood by when Washington and his compatriots finished their labors, and given utterance to their present views, would have denounced the constitution as a "covenant of blood!" They admit that it tolerates slavery, and that, while it provides for the return of fugitive slaves, it is impressively silent as to the admission of new slave states, and imposes no express duty to interfere with the subject anywhere or in any form. They admit, indeed, that it treats slavery as an affair of local sovreignty, which the people of each of the original states at least may deal with as they please, irrespective of the views and wishes of the people of other states And though they rail against its compromises, they admit too—for they cannot falsify history—that the Union could not have existed, if their spirit, instead of the spirit of peace, had prevailed. No one moreover will probably deny, that had some prophet rent the veil of the future, and revealed the time when Congress was to act in accordance with the new theories now proposed, every Southern state would have refused to join the confederacy. And suppose even that the power to enforce these theories could be found in some ambiguous clause of the constitution, and that, if exercised, an astute legal philologist might be able to maintain it. Still the question is not one of law alone, nor of philology, nor metaphysics ; but of practical statesmanship, of wise govermental expediency, of good faith, honesty and fair dealing. And we put it to you as such, and ask you again, ought the power to be exercised?

Conceded power in government is not always to be put in requisition ; doubtful power never. What a lawyer tells us we *can* do, is not an unerring test of human conduct even in the most inconsiderable affairs of private life ; but other considerations frequently remain to control the course of duty. This is peculiarly so in public affairs as to matters where the government is left free to act or forbear. Many formidable powers which Congress possesses by universal consent have been wisely suffered to remain in repose ; for example, its power over domestic commerce, and in respect to bankruptcy. On these and other subjects it has studied forbearance as the true policy of government, seldom obtruding on the field of local sovreignty, even when its power to do so was undoubted, except in accordance with some supposed and imperious public exigency, and then retiring as soon as the exigency ceased. The principle should be extended to every case where federal power may be safely dispensed with, especially if the right to interpose it is seriously doubted by intelligent men, and bad consequenccs are likely to flow from its exercise.

Nothing is clearer, fellow citizens, than that the policy of Anti-Slavery Republicanism, if prosecuted in the reckless spirit which has thus far characterised it, will lead to consequences which no one can contemplate without dismay. Other exercises of congressional power as to slavery have shown some respect to constitutional limits, to the prevailing temper and exigencies of the times, and to the issues of good or evil likely to result. Whether they were prompted by one motive or another is a question of no moment now, except with those who hope to rise and prosper by turbulent and irrelevant appeals to mere prejudice and passion. These and all other measures should be judged to-day, as they will be in-after times, by their practical adaptation to the just ends of government, and their tendency to secure the peace and well being of the country. Whatever else may be said of them, they were not animated by that spirit which, repudiating the constitutional definition of a "republican form of government," and vaunting its indifference to the fate of the Union, denounces the citizens of one section of it as the special objects of governmental "abhorrence," and asserts that the North and South are the natural enemies of each other! It was not so with the act called the Missouri Compromise, which was the result of most anxious, patient and patriotic endeavors to harmonise conflicting views, and allay for the time the frenzy of sectional strife. Nor with its repeal, which assumed tu banish the spirit of discord from the council chambers of the Nation, by limiting the range of federal action, and enlarging the domain of local sovereignty. The temper and policy of Anti-Slavery Republicanism, however, is far different. It abhors conciliation. It disdains peace. It calls back the spirit of discord. It will have nothing to do with local sovreignty of any kind, and least of all with that which looks for its warrant to the consent or choice of the people. It invokes the arm of the Nation, and proclaims congressional war —war without truce or relenting, and, for aught we see, war without end! And so sublimated are its theories that its adherents cannot advance one argument for their adoption founded on the plain principles of the constitution; nor any argument, indeed, except such as proves, if it proves anything, that slavery should be assailed everywhere, and at all times, in spite of constitutions and compacts. We invite you consider not merely the outward form of their creed, but its inner life and irrepressible practical tendencies. They ask for congressional intervention on the assumed ground that slave-holding, under all circumstances, is absolutely incompatible with religion, as well as republican principles; so much so indeed that government cannot innocently *let it alone!* And when told that the constitution was fashioned upon a different theory, they admit and lament the fact, exalt themselves above the constitution, above the government, and appeal to a "higher law!" The light by which our fathers walked and toiled will not do for them. They seek the pure empyrean! In the language of Mr. Webster, they are "above ordinances." They pant for absolute perfection, and will countenance nothing which falls short of it! On other subjects of public concern, however, they are more modest in their pretensions; peccable like other men, and far less exacting. They believe in governmental jobs, and steamships, and high tariffs, and lavish expenditures, and mortgages of revenue, and vast public debts, and all the fraudulent contrivances by which the few are enabled to enrich themselves at the expense of the many. These they can countenance and tolerate—nay, lobby for, advocate and practice—notwithstanding all their specious and hollow cant about duty, and human rights, and governmental perfection! They economise in their zeal for public purity, and would confine its benefits *wholly to the colored race!*

Congress is one of the mere agents of government. Its powers are derived from the constitution, and it has no right to act upon theories which that instrument repudiates, whether they are good or bad. Every attempt thus far to extend its control over the subject of slavery, however guarded and conciliatory, has been fraught with danger. Angry sectional controversies, alienated feeling, enfeebled patriotism, have uniformly resulted from such measures. And if this new experiment upon the public tranquility shall thrive, and all the powers of government be surrendered to Anti-Slavery Republicanism, who can tell what the future has in store for us? When one half the people of the Union shall be taught to curse it as irreligious and anti-republican, and the other half to denounce it as a fraud on their rights, an open enemy to their state policy, and their homes, who shall answer for its fate? An act of Congress passed one year may be repealed the next. You may call it a compact if you please, and declare it irrepealable; but this will not change its nature. And so the passage of every act will be only the signal light for a new mustering of hostile forces, agitation succeeding agitation with increased intensity, until every tie of fraternal feeling shall be utterly destroyed, and the blind instinct of sectional hate take the place of patriotism. Grant even that the Union is strong enough to survive the struggles of our day and generation to which this line of policy invites us. What will it be to them who shall succeed us, but a heritage of endless discord; or at best, a worthless memorial of blessings won by heroism, and lost by folly? And even for ourselves—for the interest of those now living—is it nothing to have the Nation smitten with an incurable disease; to waste it with perpetual fever, or rack it with convulsions? Will it prove to us an efficient protector while struggling against coming death, its strength emaciated, and its functions all perverted?

We are no alarmists, and are as little disposed to inspire you with unmanly fears, as to be shaken by them ourselves. The dangers of which we speak are not undefined shadows, floating in the far-off horizon of the future. They are substantial things—objects of sense—and we must deal with them. Washington saw them more than half a century ago, and in the last solemn act of his public life warned his countrymen against them. They have alarmed the patriotism of later times, and in 1839, a statesman of New York, now gone to his rest, but whose loss at this crisis is more deeply deplored than ever, addressed his fellow-citizens on the subject. And after a masterly review of the various clauses of the constitution indicating the conciliatory spirit in which the Union was formed—the clause for reclaiming fugitive slaves included—he asked:—

"Are there any who will blame our venerable fathers, the delegates in the "convention of 1787, for giving their assent to this clause of our constitu- "tion? All the old thirteen States assented to it, and to all the other con- "cessions and compromises which have been mentioned as connected with "the subject of domestic slavery. The people of all the States assented to "them, and fifty years of internal peace and abundant prosperity have at- "tested the wisdom of the Convention. What American citizen will now "rise, and claiming to be purer than Washington, the President of that con- "vention, purer and more patriotic than the sages who supported him in the "great work of forming our constitution, as they had previously in the "achievement of our Independence, will cast the first stone at the temple of "human liberty which they erected? Who that loves his country will open "again the delicate and troublesome compromises thus formed, thus settled, "and now consecrated by time and happy experience, with the hope of "reaching better results from the present temper and feeling of the country? "Who will cast upon the ocean of time and chance the invaluable blessings "we have gained, the triumph to human liberty we have secured, for the "dark and stormy prospect which presents itself of more perfect success in a "new effort? Who will wantonly trample upon the faith we have solemnly "pledged to our brethern of other States, upon entering the confederacy, in "the hope of moulding them to a more yielding disposition in some future "compact? Who will boldly strike at the Union itself, and stake its fate "against his sympathy for the slave?"—(*Address by Hon. Silas Wright, Canton; July 4th*, 1839.)

We cannot forbear, fellow-citizens, from adding to these admonitions the warning of one who was never moved by unreal danger, whose name is a passport to every democratic heart, and whose memory is revered in all lands where freedom has a shrine or a worshipper. We mean Andrew Jackson. In his farewell address to the people of the United States, he tells us :—

"The constitution cannot be maintained nor the Union preserved in oppo- "sition to public feeling, by the mere exertion of the coercive powers confi- "ded to the general government. The foundations must be laid in the affec- "tions of the people, in the security it gives to life, liberty, character and "property in every quarter of the country, and in the fraternal attachment "which the citizens of the several States bear to one another as members of "one political family, mutually contributing to promote the happiness of "each other. Hence the citizens of every State should avoid everything cal- "culated to wound the sensibilities or offend the just pride of the people of "other States; and they should frown upon any proceedings within their "own borders likely to disturb the tranquility of their political brethren in "other portions of the Union." * * * "All such efforts," he adds, "are in direct opposition to the spirit in which the Union was formed, and "must endanger its safety. Motives of philanthropy may be assigned for "this unwarrantable interference, and weak men may persuade themselves "for a moment that they are laboring in the cause of humanity, and assert-"ing the rights of the human race; but every one will see that nothing but "mischief can come from these improper assaults upon the feelings and rights "of others. Rest assured, that THE MEN FOUND BUSY IN THIS WORK OF DIS-"CORD ARE NOT WORTHY OF YOUR CONFIDENCE, AND DESERVE YOUR STRONGEST "REPROBATION."

Let us heed these impressive lessons of patriotism, and oppose those who invite us to engage with them in this new anti-slavery crusade. Reject with abhorence the treasonable fallacy that sectional strife is either wise or patriotic or necessary. Leave the people of the Territories to settle their own policy in regard to slavery. Extend to them every needed protection for the free and fair exercise of their choice, but go no further. All rational men concede—even Anti-Slavery Republicanism hesitates to deny—that when they are admitted as States, their right to establish or abolish the institution will become perfect, and no power on earth can question their decision. If they are admitted to-day with an anti-slavery constitution, they may change it to-morrow without consulting our wishes; and should Congress attempt to prevent their doing so, it would be an invasion of sovreignty, which might be lawfully resisted by force of arms. Or should they come into the Union with a constitution which prescribes no line of policy on this subject, but leaves it to be settled by State legislation afterwards, the result will be the same. And so they will have their own way at last, as we have had ours. Why not then abstain at once from all intermeddling, and stop useless agitation? We believe the people are tired of it, and desire peace. It promises no good, none whatever, but only evil, and that continually—evil in our national councils, in the different States, in churches and every where. Other and direr forms of evil will follow if we persist in urging Congress to act on theories at war alike with the constitution and common sense. Can we not afford to rely on the unwritten but steady laws of population in the disposition of questions of this kind? Have we travelled so far away from Democracy that we dare not trust the people of the territories with the management of any of their own affairs? Is no faith to be placed in the instincts and interests of intelligent men, or in anything except the coercive powers of government? Or do we really believe that all good must come to us, if at all, through acts of Congress; and that duties have no existence or validity until prescribed by statute? This, fellow citizens, is the creed of Anti-Slavery Republicanism; not of the Democratic party.

Still another party—the natural fruit, if not an essential part of the teeming diseases of the times—has been recently organized, whose creed is at war with the genius and spirit of our institutions. It seeks to veil its heresies under a specious name, and asks to be recognized as "The American Party;" though its authors chose for themselves the humbler and more apt designation of "Know-Nothings." Its creed on the slavery question is of the most plastic and accommodating kind. In the non-slaveholding portions of the country, especially in the New England States and Ohio, it agrees with Anti-Slavery Republicanism in almost every thing except the mere ascendancy of party leaders. In the slaveholding portions of the country it has endeavored, though generally without success, to gain ascendancy by professing to favor an opposite policy—a policy in accordance with prevailing local opinions. While in New York and some other places it aims to reach the seats of power by a "middle passage," or rather by being sometimes on one side and sometimes on the other; favoring each in turn without being constant to either.

So far, therefore, as it proposes to guide the actions of men or influence the course of national affairs on the subject of slavery, its creed is emphatically *know-nothing*; or rather it is a jumble of contradictions. Whether the "soldiers of fortune" who lead this enterprise shall ultimately act with or against their Whig brethren in the ranks of Anti-Slavery Republicanism, depends on time and chance; perhaps on "pay and rations." Its distinctive *mission*, to use the cant language of the day, seems to be religious instead of political, and it proposes to intervene in sectarian rather than sectional strife. Justice requires us to concede, however, that even its sectarian preferences are somewhat loose and indiscriminate; for in certain portions of the Union it is said to be Catholic, and in others Protestant. Nay, we have heard it intimated by professed adherents of the "Order" claiming to be more liberal than the rest, that in truth it had no preference for any religious sect ; nor indeed any religion at all ! Lest we should misinterpret or misunderstand its true position, and unintentionally mislead you in reference to it, we transcribe one of the oaths exacted from each member as a condition to the enjoyment of its privileges. It is in these words :—

"You promise and declare that you will support in all political matters, "for all political offices, the second degree members of this Order, provided "it be necessary for the American interests, [i. e., the interests of the "American or Know-Nothing party.] That, if it may be done legally, you "will, when elected to any office, remove all foreigners, aliens or Roman "Catholics from office; and that you will not appoint any such to office. "All this you promise and declare on your honor as Americans, to sustain "and abide by, without any hesitation or mental reservation whatever, so "help you God and keep you steadfast. You furthermore promise and de- "clare that you will not vote nor give your influence for any man for any "office in the gift of the people, unless he be an American born citizen, in "favor of American born citizens ruling America; nor if he be a Roman "Catholic. That you will not, under any circumstances, expose the name "of any member of this Order, nor reveal the existence of such an organiza- "tion. * * * * * And that you will ever seek the political advance- "ment of those men who are good and true members of this Order.

We assume that all this is meant to shadow forth some proposed line of conduct which is ultimately to take the form of governmental policy, if its authors succeed in gaining ascendancy in the Nation, as they have temporarily done in this and some other States ; and that, unlike certain rarely gifted persons whose capabilities are as apt to seek development in one direction as another, but who never accomplish anything, they have definite and substantial objects in view, and mean finally to do something. What is it ? What are their aims and purposes ? Upon what new and untried experiments do they mean to urge the government ?

The first step in their proposed line of conduct is exceedingly clear. They mean to get possession of all the offices of government, and subject all its powers to their control. To accomplish this, men are decoyed into secret places, and bound by oaths to act upon hitherto unheard of tests of political duty. Instead of swearing "not at all," or swearing to "support the constitution," they swear fealty to a self-constituted and irresponsible tribunal whose decrees are not to be examined by or known to any but the initiated. Without inquiring why these men "love darkness better than light," if it be not that "their deeds are evil," let us put another question: What right have they to cast down the time-honored democratic test of official qualification—"Is he honest? Is he capable? Is he faithful to the constitution?" And whence did they get power to substitute that other test—"Is he a good and true member of this Order? Is he an American born citizen? Is he Protestant? Is he Catholic?"

The federal constitution declares that "no *religious* test shall ever be required as a qualification to any office or public trust, under the United States." A commentator upon that instrument who has won an imperishable name in the world of letters as well as jurisprudence, Mr. Justice Story, explains the object of the clause thus:

"The framers of the constitution were fully sensible of the dangers from this source, marked out in the history of other ages and countries, and not wholly unknown to our own. They knew that bigotry was unceasingly vigilant in its stratagems to secure to itself an exclusive ascendancy over the human mind, and that intolerance was ever ready to arm itself with all the terrors of the civil power to exterminate those who doubted its dogmas or resisted its infallibility. The Catholic and Protestant had alternately waged the most ferocious and unrelenting warfare on each other, and Protestantism itself, at the very moment it was proclaiming the right of private judgment, prescribed boundaries to that right, beyond which if any dared to pass he must seal his rashness with the blood of martyrdom. The history of the parent country, too, could not fail to instruct them in the use and abuses of religious tests. They there found the pains and penalties of non-conformity written in no equivocal language, and enforced with a stern and vindictive jealousy. * * * It is easy to foresee that, without some prohibition of religious tests, a successful sect in our country might, by once possessing power, pass test laws which would secure to themselves *a monopoly of all the offices of trust and profit under the national government.*"

The authors and abettors of Know-Nothingism may not have read Judge Story, but it is entirely clear that *he has read them.* And however anxious they may be to veil their real designs from the men now living, they were not hid from our fathers. Those designs, so far as they relate to the practical application of a religious test of official qualification, are not only directly at war with the genius of the constitution, but with its plain words. The Democratic Party repudiates all such heresies ; nay, abhors them. It believes with Jefferson, that opinions of every kind may be tolerated by a government which leaves reason free to combat them. It says with Milton—" Let truth and falsehood grapple. Who ever knew truth put to the worse in a free and open encounter ?" It holds with the constitution, that no man should be subject to political disabilities, persecution or any other penalty, on account of his religious belief; that to invoke organized political action for such a purpose is unwise and unjust not only, but absurd. It unchains the mind, throws wide open the portals of truth, and bids all enter, seek and find. And it tells them to rely on government for protection in the pursuit of their object, so long as they aim at private ends, and do not invade the rights of others. But when they form themselves into political parties, and claim to control the course of public affairs, they must subordinate their theories to those of the government, or be content to be numbered among its enemies. Let the advocates and adherents of Know-Nothingism remember, that just so far as they seek to gain or monopolize power by the application of religious tests, they, like Anti-Slavery Republicanism, repudiate the constitution, and affirm that there is a "higher law" for governmental agents and politicians.

The intolerance of Know-Nothingism, however, reaches far beyond what we have mentioned, and brings the Protestant as well as Catholic within its interdicting curse. It binds each of its members, as we have seen, "not to vote or give his influence for any man, for any office in the gift of the people, unless he be an *American born citizen*;" and even then he is to be prescribed, unless, in addition, he is "in favor of American born citizens ruling America !" The man who, like Lafayette, Kosciusko, Montgomery, De Kalb, Steuben, or Hamilton, was born in a foreign land, is to be disqualified from holding office for that reason alone ; though he has been admitted to all the rights of citizenship under the constitution and laws of the United States. No matter whether his religious belief is in accordance with the prescribed standard or not, nor how long he has lived among us, nor what may be his intelligence, or his titles to public respect or gratitude: nay, though he has been attracted hither by the purest devotion to the cause of Republican liberty, and has offered his blood as a sacrifice upon its altars. All this is nothing, for he is not an American by *birth!* The Order sits in judgment upon his nativity, finds him guilty of being born in the wrong place, and condemns him to civil banishment! And so even though his stars were propitious, and he was born in strict accordance with the decrees of the Order, on American soil; still he is to be proscribed, unless he unites with its leaders in advocating intolerance; in other words, unless he satisfies them that he is *in favor* of excluding all but American born citizens from office!

Let us remind you again that the creed of every political party which is truly loyal to government, and means to act under it, and not against it, will always be found in harmony with its fundamental principles. And we ask all candid men who have been incautiously lured into the ranks of Know-Nothingism, to re-examine its distinctive doctrines, and compare them with those embodied in the constitution. They will be found in direct antagonism to each other. The constitution strives to banish the spirit of religious intolerance in government as alien to the true principles of civil liberty; while Know-Nothingism erects an altar to it, and compels men to bow down and worship it! The constitution declares that all citizens are eligible to office, irrespective of the accident of birth, except the office of President; but Know-Nothingism denounces this as unwise, and arrays itself in open opposition to it! The constitution tells each officer and agent of government to look to its precepts and doctrines for the rule and measure of public duty; while Know-Nothingism commands them to look for guidance to the counsels and decrees of politicians! The constitution moreover favors publicity in all organized efforts to influence the action of government, and submits them to the ordeal of public scrutiny; while Know-Nothingism shrouds itself in congenial darkness, plots in secret, and forbids scrutiny!

If the Know-Nothing and Anti-Slavery Republican parties, or any other class of men in the community, are dissatisfied with our present form of government, and wish to change its organic structure, no one denies their right to attempt it by fair means. Let them take the open field, and tell the people plainly that this is their purpose. The citizen will then know what to expect from them, and be prepared to act accordingly. But to make their way to place and power under the false pretence that they are friends of the constitution, that they believe in its principles, and mean to act in accordance with its spirit, while secretly repudiating its fundamental teachings, is neither manly nor honest.

We have forborne to speak of a third class of men who have been misled into false views of the nature and true office of government. We mean those who, within the last year or two, organized themselves into a political party to enforce the single virtue of Temperance, leaving the other virtues to shift for themselves. After urging our State Legislature to disregard the constitution by passing a law in violation of it—a law the authorship of which none of its followers are willing to avow—it has quietly subsided, along with the waning remnant of the old Abolition party, into the ranks of Anti-Slavery Republicanism. Both will be remembered hereafter for their good intentions, their bad deeds, and their ignoble end.

Fellow-citizens, the parties of which we have spoken have originated in one common error—an error into which the Democratic Party can never fall until it renounces its ancient faith. They have mistaken the proper ends of political association, and the true office and limits of human government. While professing to act under the constitution, and in accordance with its spirit, they have exalted themselves above it, and appealed to a "higher law." Their respective creeds assume that neither the guidance of reason, the lights of education, the injunctions of religion, nor the promptings of a wise self-interest, can be relied on in any relation of life. Philanthropy must be taught by act of Congress, or men will never practice it! Religion must be controlled by politicians, or heresy will be the order of the day! And unless Temperance is hunted down by policemen, and hedged in with penalties, it can never be secured! The entire field of human endeavor must be scanned with anxious care, not to find how much of it can be safely left to individual freedom and responsibility, but how far Government can encroach on it! Its intermeddling hand must be seen and felt everywhere and at all times, constantly trenching on those moral agencies, which—guided by a Power wiser and more benificent than that of politicians—are silently influencing the course of human conduct and shaping the destinies of men and nations.

We believe it may be said with confidence that if the Democratic party has ever deviated into errors like those to which we have alluded, it has not persevered in them. It cannot do so without being false to its own principles. Reflecting and patriotic men everywhere acknowledge the value of its past achievments, and admit that its services were never needed more than at this hour. They are not needed to guard any one interest of the country, but every one; to maintain our written constitutions, which, under Providence, protect us all; and to secure and perpetuate the blessings of sound and wise administration. They will be needed in all coming vicissitudes, whether of war or peace, adversity or prosperity. It is almost the only association of men, political or religious, which sectional strife and fanaticism have not utterly prostrated; certainly the only one which has power to cast upon the political evils which afflict the Nation and menace its life. Let its once victorious legions be again summoned to the field of controversy. Let its voice go forth as of old, cheering the hearts, and arousing the courage, and re-animating the hopes of his friends. And let every one who has named its name and professed its faith in former years, strive with earnestness and singleness of purpose for the attainment of these ends; remembering that "a house divided against itself cannot stand."

Mr. Shepard, from the committee for that purpose, reported the following resolutions:

Resolved, That our Federal Government being restrained by the Constitution to specific functions, the legitimate province of national politics is confined within the same limits; and that every popular agitation or movement that aims to transcend these constitutional bounds, and to avail itself of the organic force of government to accomplish its purposes, is a perversion of the uses and objects of party, tending to great and serious usurpations in government, and when unjustly enforced against any particular section of the country is a tyranny that should be resisted by all good citizens.

Resolved, That the agitation of the slavery question by the people of the non-slaveholding States, with a view to impair the security of the domestic institutions of the South, whether pursued in demonstrations by political conventions or by discussion and legislation in Congress, falls within this category; and that the experience of the past has shown that, while it has compassed no good, it has resulted in serious evils, weakening the brotherhood of the States, and that mutual and unconstrained association that was once their chief bond of union, and substituting in their place the domineering influence of political parties and the coercive power of the Federal Government.

Resolved, That the recent manifestation of this evil spirit in the organization of the so-called Republican party, by showing to what a treasonable head it has already arrived, demonstrates the unfortunate tendency of all its antecedent steps in this agitation. And that we point to its avowed doctrine of hostility to the Constitution, its imputation upon the spirit in which it originated, its denial of the equality of the States, and its invocation of a higher law than the Constitution, and its whole scheme of civil discord to be accomplished by political usurpation, as the natural result and consummation of the latetudinarian doctrines and false and erroneous policy which, since the foundation of the government, have characterised the creed of the opponents of the Democracy.

Resolved, That the determination of Congress, avowed in the Kansas-Nebraska bill, to reject from the national councils the subject of slavery in the Territories, and to leave the people thereof free to regulate their domestic institutions in their own way, subject only to the Constitution of the United States, is one that accords with the sentiments of the Democracy of this State, and with the traditional course of legislation by Congress, which, under democratic auspices, has gradually in successive territorial bills extended the domain of popular rights, and limited the range of congressional action. And that we believe this disposition of the question will result most auspiciously to the peace of the Union, and the cause of good government.

Resolved, That (in the language of the recent message of President Pierce to Congress) "the people of the Territory by its organic law possessing the right to determine their domestic institutions, are entitled, while deporting themselves peacefully, to the free exercise of that right, and must be protected in the enjoyment of it, without interference on the part of the citizens of any of the States."

"*Resolved*, That the Democracy of the State of New York deem this a fit "occasion to tender to their fellow citizens of the whole Union, their heart- "felt congratulations on the triumph, in the recent elections in several of "the Northern, Eastern and Western, as well as Southern States, of the "principles of the Kansas-Nebraska bill and the doctrines of civil and religious "liberty which have been so violently assailed by a secret political order known "as the Know-Nothing party; and we hold it to be our highest duty to con-

"tinue our efforts in the maintenance and defence of those principles and the "constitutional rights of every faction and every class of citizens against "their opponents of every description, whether the so-called Republicans, "Know-Nothings or Fusionists; and to this end we look with confidence to "the support and support and approbation of all good and true men—friends "to the Constitution and the Union throughout the country."

Resolved, That though we have encountered in the field of politics for upwards of twenty years, as our determined and most effective opponent, the Whig party, we cannot forbear the expression of our regret at its death. And we deem it due to the memory of a gallant adversary to say, that its open and manly warfare, the national scope of its principles, and the high tone and ability of its leaders, made it an antagonist worthy of the democracy; and that the record of its life contrasts well with that of the secret, sectional, and narrow-minded factions which have succeeded it, and which claim to divide its political inheritance.

Resolved, That the administration of President Pierce has merited the approval of the Democracy of this State and the Union, manifesting as it has on every occasion in which the national honor has been involved, a most patriotic and determined spirit, exhibiting in all its departments, vigilance, energy and rigid probity, protecting the treasury from the corrupt combinations of Congress by the exercise of the veto power, and maintaining the cause of democracy by the enunciation of sound opinion and the example of good government and wise measures.

Resolved, That the delegates selected by this Convention to represent the State of New York in the National Convention, are hereby instructed to cast the vote of this State as a unit, and that a majority of the delegates are hereby authorised to fill all vacancies occurring in their body.

The question was taken on the Address and it was adopted. (Messrs. VAN DYCK and BURT voting in the negative.)

A division being called for on the Resolutions, they were adopted; the first, third and fifth, seventh, eighth and ninth, unanimously, and the second, fourth and sixth with two dissenting votes—Messrs. VAN DYCK and BURT.

The Convention then adjourned till 9 A. M. of Friday.

FRIDAY, January 12.

The Convention met to hear the report of the committee appointed to nominate to it Delegates to the National Democratic Convention. The Committee reported the following names which were adopted by acclamation:

DELEGATES AT LARGE.

HORATIO SEYMOUR, NICHOLAS HILL, Jr.,
DEAN RICHMOND, ROBERT KELLY.

District Delegates.

District.

I.—William H. Ludlow, Henry Floyd Jones.
II.—Samuel E. Johnson, Thomas G. Tallmadge.
III.—Thomas Burns, Albert Smith.
IV.—John Kelly, George H. Purser.
V.—Stephen H. Feeks, Wilson Small.
VI.—Isaac V. Fowler, John Cochrane.
VII.—William D. Kennedy, William J. Peck.
VIII.—Lorenzo B. Shepard, Daniel F. Tieman.
IX.—James Conner, Azor B. Crane.
X.—John C. Holly, David E. Fowler.
XI.—T. R. Westbrook, Danforth K. Olney.
XII.—John P. Beekman, Gilbert Dean.
XIII.—William A. Beach, Charles L. McArthur.
XIV.—John V. L. Pruyn, John McKnight.
XV.—Isaac Bishop, Joshua M. Todd.
XVI.—Timothy Hoyle, Augustus C. Hand.
XVII.—John L. Russell, William C. Crain.
XVIII.—John C. Wright, Elias A. Brown.
XIX.—Robert Parker, Samuel M. Shaw.
XX.—John Stryker, Francis Kernan.
XXI.—Horatio Ballard, Horace G. Prindle.
XXII.—Sands N. Kenyon, Sidney T. Fairchild.
XXIII.—De Witt C. West, Charles Smith.
XXIV.—Dennis McCarthy, Seth Hutchinson.
XXV.—Ellmore P. Ross, Cullen Foster.
XXVI.—William C. Dryer, Charles Sentell,
XXVII.—John J. Taylor, Henry D. Barto, Jr.
XXVIII.—William C. Rhodes, James Faulkner.
XXIX.—Simeon B. Jewett, James C. Campbell.
XXX.—Henry J. Glowacki, L. P. Weatheby.
XXXI.—William Vandervoort, Orson Tousley.
XXXII.—Israel T. Hatch, James M. Humphrey.
XXXIII.—Lemuel S. Jenks, Niran Sackett.

On motion of WM. A. CARPENTER, of Columbia, the following resolution was also unanimously adopted:

Resolved, That any delegate appointed to the National Convention, who may be found to belong to, or affiliate with the organization commonly known as the Know Nothing organization, shall be declared by the delegation to be incompetent to act as delegate, and the vacancy caused by such removal, shall be filled in the manner provided by the resolution of the Convention.

The Convention then directed that the proceedings of the Convention be published.

The usual resolution of thanks to the Officers of the Convention was then passed; and with cheers for the Platform and the Delegation the Convention ADJOURNED.

WILLIAM H. LUDLOW,
President.

GEORGE H. PURSER,
JOSEPH MARTIN,
ALONZO MCCONIHE,
JOHN L. RUSSELL,
GEORGE B. JUDD,
CHARLES MCLEAN,
JAMES FAULKNER,
A. V. E. HOTCHKISS,
Vice Presidents.

LEVI H. BROWN,
H. P. CLINTON,
HIRAM ENGLE,
HORACE PACKER,
Secretaries.

CONSOLIDATION OF THE ARGUS & ATLAS.

Mr. Comstock having purchased the interest of Mr. Johnson in the Argus, and Mr. Cassidy that of Mr. Van Dyck in the Atlas, they have effected an arrangement for the consolidation of the two papers under the name of THE ATLAS & ARGUS, and for conducting the Newspaper and the Job Printing Establishment connected therewith, as sole Proprietors, under the co-partnership designation of COMSTOCK & CASSIDY.

The Proprietors cannot be mistaken in saying that the union of the two Democratic Papers at the Capitol, had long been regarded by Democrats of the State, as essential to the restoration and perpetuation of harmony, and the renewal and continuance of strength and vigor in their party. Formidable obstacles have hitherto stood in the way of such a consummation, and they have not now been surmounted except by the exercise of a considerable degree of patience and perseverance, the active exertions of friends, and the assumption by the proprietors of no inconsiderable pecuniary responsibilities. They think they do not mistake the Democratic sentiment of the State, when they confidently trust to it for an appreciation of the motives of their action, and for protection and support in this enterprise.

The consolidated paper probably commences with a larger subscription list—having reference to all its editions—than any other Democratic paper in the Union. But it is by no means as large as a proper remuneration for the sacrifices connected with bringing the two establishments together and an efficient support of the paper, as well as a vigorous advocacy of Democratic principles in this section of the Union, require. The proprietors believe that if their political friends—and they include in the term all who intend to act with the Democratic party of the nation—will co-operate with them, this paper may have an ample support, and, it will perhaps not be deemed a lack of modesty on their part to add, may render important service in securing the triumph of the doctrines and candidates of the Democratic party.

May they not appeal to their political friends and remind them that a favorable opportunity—one which has not been afforded for years—is now presented for placing a newspaper at the Capitol of the State on a permanent and influential basis, and of thus contributing whatever may be done through such an agency, to the strength, consolidation, and permanency of the party? They respectfully ask the co-operation of Democrats in extending the circulation of The Atlas & Argus.

TERMS FOR THE ALBANY ATLAS & ARGUS.

TERMS FOR SINGLE SUBSCRIPTIONS.

ATLAS & ARGUS (Daily)—Eight dollars per annum, payable half yearly, or *seven dollars if paid in advance.*

ATLAS & ARGUS (Semi-Weekly)—Four dollars per annum, payable half yearly, or *three dollars if paid in advance.*

ATLAS & ARGUS (Weekly)—One dollar and fifty cents per annum invariably, unless paid in advance. *If paid in advance one dollar.*

☞ No new subscriptions for the Weekly will be received unless paid in advance.

SPECIAL TERMS FOR PACKAGES.

To any one who will send us Ten subscribers for the Daily, with payment in advance, ($70,) we will send a copy of the Daily for one year.

To any one who will send us Ten subscribers for the Semi-Weekly, and payment in advance, ($30,) we will send a copy of the Semi-Weekly for one year.

To any person who will send us Ten subscribers for the Weekly—*the packages to be sent to one address*—and payment in advance, ($10,) a copy of the Weekly for one year.

www.ingramcontent.com/pod-product-compliance
Lightning Source LLC
LaVergne TN
LVHW011125110826
845150LV00008B/2257
9781418194840